~ Purchased
with interest income
from the
library's trust fund ~

National Landmarks

# The Lincoln Memorial

by Kathleen W. Deady

**Consultant:**
Marilyn Harper
Historian
National Park Service, Retired
Washington, D.C.

## Bridgestone Books
an imprint of Capstone Press
Mankato, Minnesota

Bridgestone Books are published by Capstone Press
151 Good Counsel Drive, P.O. Box 669, Mankato, Minnesota 56002
http://www.capstone-press.com

*Library of Congress Cataloging-in-Publication Data*
Deady, Kathleen W.
    The Lincoln Memorial/by Kathleen W. Deady.
    p. cm.—(National landmarks)
    Includes bibliographical references (p. 23) and index.
    Summary: Discusses the history of the Lincoln Memorial, its designer, construction of
    the monument, its location, and its importance to the people of the United States.
    ISBN 0-7368-1114-1
    1. Lincoln Memorial (Washington, D.C.)—Juvenile literature. 2. Lincoln Memorial
(Washington, D.C.)—History—Juvenile literature. 3. Lincoln, Abraham, 1809–1865—
Monuments—Juvenile literature. 4. Washington (D.C.)—Buildings, structures, etc.—Juvenile
literature. [1. Lincoln Memorial (Washington, D.C.) 2. National monuments.]
I. Title. II. Series.
F203.4.L73 D4 2002
975.3—dc21                                                                    2001003302

**Editorial Credits**

Erika Mikkelson, editor; Karen Risch, product planning editor; Linda Clavel, cover designer
    and interior layout designer; Erin Scott, SARIN Creative, illustrator; Alta Schaffer,
    photo researcher

**Photo Credits**

Archive Photos, 10
Digital Stock, cover, 1, 4, 6, 20
Library of Congress, 8, 12
Michael Evans/The Image Finders, 14
Stock Montage, Inc., 16, 18

1 2 3 4 5 6 07 06 05 04 03 02

# Table of Contents

# Fast Facts

* **Construction Materials:** The outside of the Lincoln Memorial is made of Colorado Yule marble. The inside is made of Indiana limestone. The ceiling is made of Alabama marble. The floor is made of pink Tennessee marble.

* **Height:** The memorial stands 80 feet (24 meters) tall.

* **Width:** The memorial is 118 ⅔ feet (36.2 meters) wide.

* **Length:** The memorial is 189 feet (58 meters) long.

* **Statue of Lincoln:** The statue inside the memorial is 19 feet (5.8 meters) tall. It was carved from 28 blocks of Georgian marble.

* **Date Built:** Work on the memorial started in 1914. It was completed in 1922.

* **Cost:** The Lincoln Memorial cost about $3 million.

* **Visitors:** More than 3 million people visit the memorial every year. The Lincoln Memorial is one of the most popular tourist spots in Washington, D.C.

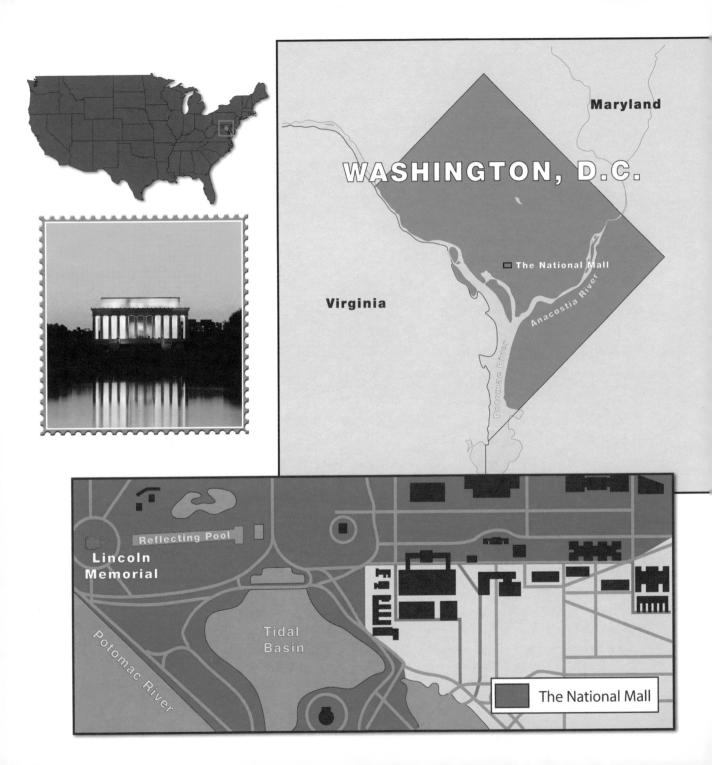

Maryland

WASHINGTON, D.C.

Virginia

Anacostia River

Potomac River

□ The National Mall

Reflecting Pool

Lincoln
Memorial

Tidal
Basin

Potomac River

The National Mall

# The Lincoln Memorial

The Lincoln Memorial honors President Abraham Lincoln. This monument reminds people of a great leader in the history of the United States.

The Lincoln Memorial is in Washington, D.C., near the Potomac River. It stands at the west end of the National Mall. This large park spreads across many blocks in the middle of Washington, D.C.

The Lincoln Memorial is a huge marble building. It sits on a raised terrace, or platform. Columns surround the building. A marble stairway leads to the entrance. The entrance faces east. A long reflecting pool lies in front of the memorial.

The memorial has three rooms. The center room holds a large statue of Lincoln sitting in a chair. Lincoln's most famous speeches are carved in stone in the northern and southern rooms. Murals showing Lincoln's life are above the speeches.

**The Lincoln Memorial is in Washington, D.C.**

# Abraham Lincoln

Abraham Lincoln became president on March 4, 1861. In April, the Civil War (1861–1865) started between the Northern and the Southern states. The South wanted strong state governments. The North wanted a strong federal government. The South also wanted slavery to remain legal. But many people in the North thought slavery was wrong.

Lincoln worked to keep the nation together. He thought people should be free and equal. In 1863, he signed the Emancipation Proclamation. This new law said slaves in the South were free.

On March 4, 1865, Lincoln began his second term as president. He gave a speech called his "Second Inaugural Address." He spoke about peace and forgiveness.

The Civil War ended in April 1865. The United States remained together as one nation. Some people did not like Lincoln's ideas. On April 14, John Wilkes Booth shot Lincoln. Lincoln died the next day, April 15, 1865.

**Abraham Lincoln was the 16th president of the United States.**

After Lincoln's death, many people wanted to build a memorial to honor him. Many Americans believed he was a great leader. He had worked hard for peace and freedom.

In 1867, Congress formed the Lincoln Monument Association to plan the memorial. A sculptor named Clark Mills made a design. He planned a huge raised statue of Lincoln with soldiers around it. But Congress did not set aside money for the memorial. The project never was started.

Illinois Senator Shelby Cullom tried for years to restart the project. Cullom finally received support from Illinois Representative Joseph Cannon. They asked Congress to give money for a memorial.

In February 1911, Congress passed a bill to form the Lincoln Memorial Commission. Congress set aside $2 million. This was the most money ever granted for a monument. The commission then could begin planning the memorial.

**Illinois Senator Shelby Cullom wanted a memorial in Washington, D.C., to honor Abraham Lincoln.**

PLAN of the City of WASHINGTON.

Georges Town

POTOMAK RIVER

EASTERN BRANCH

Capitol 38. 55. N.

# New Ideas

By 1911, the United States had changed. People had new ideas for a monument. People were driving cars. One senator suggested building a memorial highway lined with statues and historical signs. Others suggested creating a park or a huge arch. But the commission wanted a grand building with a statue of Lincoln inside.

People thought of a location for the memorial. Someone suggested the east bank of the Potomac River. Others thought this area, called Potomac Flats, was a bad location. It was a recently drained swamp.

But the commission liked the idea. A French engineer named Pierre Charles L'Enfant had designed Washington. He planned a long, grassy mall, or park, from east to west. He wanted trees and national monuments on the Mall. The capitol building was already at the east end. The Washington Monument stood in the middle. The commission thought a grand building at the west end would be perfect.

**Pierre Charles L'Enfant drew this map. It was his original plan for the city of Washington, D.C.**

# Designing the Lincoln Memorial

The commission chose architect Henry Bacon to design the memorial. He wanted the memorial to be different from others in Washington, D.C. Bacon had studied in Europe. He liked ancient Greek buildings. Bacon designed the memorial in the style of a famous Greek temple called the Parthenon.

Bacon designed 36 columns around the outside of the building. They represent the 36 states in the country when Lincoln died. The names of 48 states are above the columns. These states made up the country when the memorial was completed in 1922. Later, a plaque was added to include Alaska and Hawaii.

Bacon designed three rooms. The center room has a statue of Lincoln. The other rooms display Lincoln's speeches. The commission chose the "Second Inaugural Address" and the "Gettysburg Address." Lincoln gave this famous speech on November 19, 1863, in Gettysburg, Pennsylvania. He said the government should be run by the people, for the people.

**The statue of Lincoln sits in the memorial's center room.**

Workers began building the memorial on February 12, 1914. This date would have been Abraham Lincoln's 105th birthday. Workers first built a strong foundation. They secured thick concrete posts deep into the solid rock below the soft ground. In 1915, they started the building itself. Workers used marble from several states.

Daniel Chester French created the statue of Lincoln. He carved the statue from 28 blocks of Georgian marble. Ernest C. Bairstow carved Lincoln's speeches into the walls. Jules Guerin painted murals above the speeches.

Work slowed in 1917. The United States was fighting in World War I (1914–1918). Many workers stopped working on the building to serve in the war.

Workers finished the roof in 1918. In 1920, the statue was placed in the building. Workers then started making the reflecting pool. Workers finished the memorial in 1922. The final cost was $3 million.

**The Lincoln Memorial is made out of marble from several U.S. states.**

# The Lincoln Memorial Dedication

The Lincoln Memorial opened to the public on May 30, 1922. This date was about 57 years after Abraham Lincoln died. About 50,000 people came to honor Lincoln. Thousands more people listened to the speeches on radios in their homes.

Many important people were at the ceremony. The guest of honor was Lincoln's only surviving son, Robert Todd Lincoln. President Warren Harding spoke of how Lincoln united the country. Former President William Howard Taft spoke of Lincoln's courage, kindness, and patience.

An African American man named Robert Moton also spoke. Moton was the principal of Tuskegee Institute, a college for African American students. He spoke of Lincoln's efforts for freedom and equality. Moton urged Americans to finish Lincoln's work by gaining equal rights for all people.

**People celebrated the dedication of the Lincoln Memorial on May 30, 1922.**

# Visiting the Lincoln Memorial

People gather at the Lincoln Memorial for many events. Marian Anderson was a famous African American opera singer. In 1939, Anderson stood on the memorial's steps and sang to 75,000 people.

In 1963, more than 200,000 people came to Washington, D.C. They demanded that the government pass a civil rights bill. Dr. Martin Luther King Jr. gave his famous "I Have a Dream" speech at the Lincoln Memorial. He said he wanted freedom and equal rights for all people.

Weather and the environment have damaged the memorial over the years. In 1993, workers began to repair the damage. They restored the murals and fixed the walkway. They replaced the memorial's roof. Today, workers continue to fix the memorial.

The Lincoln Memorial has become a symbol of freedom. More than 3 million people visit the memorial every year. They remember Abraham Lincoln and the work he did for the United States.

**Millions of people visit the Lincoln Memorial each year.**

# Important Dates

★ 1860—Abraham Lincoln is elected 16th President of the United States.

★ 1861—Lincoln begins his first term as president on March 4.
   The Civil War begins on April 12.

★ 1863—Lincoln signs the Emancipation Proclamation to free the slaves in the South.

★ 1865—Lincoln begins his second term as president on March 4. He gives his Second Inaugural Address. The Civil War ends on April 9. John Wilkes Booth shoots Lincoln on April 14. Lincoln dies April 15.

★ 1867—People want to build a memorial to honor Lincoln. But there is no money for the project.

★ 1911—Congress sets aside $2 million for a memorial to Lincoln.

★ 1914—Workers start to build the Lincoln Memorial.

★ 1922—Workers finish building the Lincoln Memorial. People hold a dedication ceremony. They officially open the Lincoln Memorial to the public.

★ 1963—Dr. Martin Luther King Jr. gives his famous "I Have a Dream" speech at the Lincoln Memorial.

★ 1993–present—Workers repair damage to the Lincoln Memorial.

# Words to Know

**column** (CAWL-um)—a tall post that helps support a building

**democracy** (de-MAWK-kri-see)—a country with a government run by the people

**Gettysburg Address** (GET-eez-burg ad-DRESS)—a speech Abraham Lincoln gave in Gettysburg, Pennsylvania on November 19, 1863

**Inaugural Address** (in-AW-ger-ul ad-DRESS)—the speech a president gives when he or she is sworn into office

**reflecting pool** (ri-FLEK-ting POOL)—a large, shallow pool of still water; a reflecting pool lies in front of the Lincoln Memorial.

**sculptor** (SKUHLP-tur)—an artist who carves statues out of stone, wood, or other materials

**senator** (SEN-ah-tur)—a person elected to represent the people and serve in the government

**slavery** (SLAY-vur-ee)—the owning of other people; slaves are forced to work without pay.

# Read More

**Binns, Tristan Boyer**. *The Lincoln Memorial.* Symbols of Freedom. Chicago: Heinemann Library, 2001.

**Gilmore, Frederic.** *The Lincoln Memorial: A Great President Remembered.* Chanhassen, Minn.: Child's World, 2001.

# Useful Addresses

**National Capital Parks—
  The National Mall**
900 Ohio Drive SW
Washington, DC  20024-2000

**National Park Service—
  National Capital Region**
1100 Ohio Drive SW
Washington, DC  20242

# Internet Sites

**Lincoln Memorial**
http://www.nps.gov/linc/home.htm
**The Lincoln Memorial**
http://library.thinkquest.org/17188/lincoln.html?tqskip=1
**Monuments and Memorials—Lincoln Memorial**
http://www.kreative.net/cooper/TourOfDC/monuments/
  lincoln-memorial

# Index